The Junior Text - Book

A Manual of Questions And Answers On
Junior Christian Endeavor Work
For Superintendents And Members
Of Junior Societies Of
Christian Endeavor

By Amos R. Wells

Editorial Secretary of the United
Society of Christian Endeavor and
Author of "The Junior Manual," etc.

First Fruits Press
Wilmore, Kentucky
c2015

The junior text-book: a manual of questions and answers on Junior Christian Endeavor work, by Amos R. Wells.

First Fruits Press, ©2015
Previously published: Boston and Chicago: United Society of Christian Endeavor, ©1911.

ISBN: 9781621713913 (print), 9781621713920 (digital)

Digital version at http://place.asburyseminary.edu/christianendeavorbooks/14/

First Fruits Press is a digital imprint of the Asbury Theological Seminary, B.L. Fisher Library. Asbury Theological Seminary is the legal owner of the material previously published by the Pentecostal Publishing Co. and reserves the right to release new editions of this material as well as new material produced by Asbury Theological Seminary. Its publications are available for noncommercial and educational uses, such as research, teaching and private study. First Fruits Press has licensed the digital version of this work under the Creative Commons Attribution Noncommercial 3.0 United States License. To view a copy of this license, visit http://creativecommons.org/licenses/by-nc/3.0/us/.

For all other uses, contact:

First Fruits Press
B.L. Fisher Library
Asbury Theological Seminary
204 N. Lexington Ave.
Wilmore, KY 40390
http://place.asburyseminary.edu/firstfruits

Wells, Amos R. (Amos Russel), 1862-1933.
    The junior text-book : a manual of questions and answers on Junior Christian Endeavor work / by Amos R. Wells.
    100 pages ; 21 cm.
    Wilmore, Ky. : First Fruits Press, ©2015.
    "For superintendents and members of Junior Societies of Christian Endeavor."
    Reprint. Previously published: Boston : United Society of Christian Endeavor, ©1911.
    ISBN: 9781621713913 (pbk.)
    1. International Society of Christian Endeavor. 2. Christian education of young people -- Handbooks, manuals, etc. I. Title.
BV1426 .W48 2015

Cover design by Jonathan Ramsay

asburyseminary.edu
800.2ASBURY
204 North Lexington Avenue
Wilmore, Kentucky 40390

First Fruits
THE ACADEMIC OPEN PRESS OF ASBURY SEMINARY

First Fruits Press
The Academic Open Press of Asbury Theological Seminary
204 N. Lexington Ave., Wilmore, KY 40390
859-858-2236
first.fruits@asburyseminary.edu
asbury.to/firstfruits

The Junior Text-Book

The
Junior Text-Book

A Manual of Questions and Answers on
Junior Christian Endeavor Work
for Superintendents and Members
of Junior Societies of
Christian Endeavor

By AMOS R. WELLS

*Editorial Secretary of the United Society of Christian Endeavor
and Author of " The Junior Manual," etc.*

BOSTON AND CHICAGO
UNITED SOCIETY OF CHRISTIAN ENDEAVOR

How To Use This Book

The various chapters of this book are published as separate leaflets, and are sold by the United Society of Christian Endeavor either separately or in quantities. It is recommended that Junior societies obtain a supply of them sufficient to give every member of the society a copy of each of the first three leaflets (Chapters I., II., and III. of this book), and that every officer and committee member receive the leaflet discussing his work. A copy of the leaflet for prayer-meeting leaders (Chapter XX.) may well be placed in the hands of the successive leaders of your meetings, and the leaflet for preparatory members (Chapter XXI.) may be given to those members. The leaflets on the Quiet Hour and the Tenth Legion are for general distribution when it is desired to arouse special interest in these subjects.

It is hoped that the societies everywhere will adopt a rule that each officer and committee member shall, within a month after election, pass (75%) an examination in the work of his office, or else cease to hold it. The questions given here will be asked by the superintendent, and it is partly for the superintendent's convenience that the leaflets have been gathered into the present volume.

Also, many superintendents will wish to form the older Juniors into classes for the study of this book, that they may become acquainted with all lines of Junior work. The officers of the society, especially, should take this course; so should the Junior committee of the Young People's society. All members of such a class should have copies of the text-book.

Conferences of Junior workers are often held in connection with Christian Endeavor conventions and summer schools. Classes in Junior methods may well be formed at such times, and this book will serve as a convenient and comprehensive text-book. The questions and answers will serve as bases of discussion, and essays and talks on topics suggested by these studies will be assigned by the leader according to the time at the disposal of the class.

AMOS R. WELLS.

Boston.

Contents

CHAPTER I

The Prayer Meeting

What is the purpose of a prayer meeting?

To talk together about the highest and most important things, to show others that we love Christ, to pray to Christ and sing His praises and learn about Him, and to receive the help that He always gives those who meet together in His name.

Why should we take part in the prayer meeting?

Because we have promised to do so, and we have promised because taking part in prayer meeting will strengthen us, help us, and please Christ.

How will our taking part in prayer meeting strengthen us?

It will give us confidence in ourselves. It will develop our powers of speaking in public and quicken our minds. It will train us for work in the older part of the church. It will make us more successful when we go out to do a man's or a woman's work in the world. Best of all, it will strengthen our good purposes and make us better and wiser.

How will our taking part in prayer meeting help others?

It will show them that we are trying to follow Christ, and so will give them courage to lead the Christian life. It will show them how to do work in the Junior society, and so help them to grow.

How will our taking part in the prayer meeting please Christ?

He wants us to be strong, manly Christians. He is glad to have us show that we love Him and are trying to do His will. He can come nearer to us when thus we try to get close to Him.

How can we overcome timidity in the meetings?

By remembering that Christ is ready to help us, and by forgetting about every one but His kind, loving presence. Also by remembering that we are not afraid of this Junior and that Junior — not afraid of any one of them separately. Why, then, should we be afraid of them all together?

How can we prepare to take part in the meeting?

We should begin our preparation for the next meeting as soon as the last one is over. We should read the subject of the meeting, and then the Bible verses given, and carry them in our minds, thinking them over and asking Jesus to give us some helpful thought on the subject. If we keep our minds upon the subject we are quite sure to read something or see something or hear something or think of something that will give a helpful thought to express in the meeting.

What is the first step in taking part in the meeting?

We may read a Bible verse or some other quotation. We should read it over often beforehand and become quite familiar with it. In the meeting we should read it loudly, so that all may hear.

What is the next step?

[11]

To commit a Bible verse or a quotation to memory, and repeat it, rather than read it.

What is the next step?

To add something of our own to the quotation, though it is only a sentence telling how it has helped us and what use we have made of it.

What is the next step?

To give a sentence prayer. At first we may commit to memory some of the Bible prayers— the Psalms are full of them; then we shall go on to offer little prayers of our own.

What is the purpose of our prayer-meeting work?

To please Jesus and do His will.

CHAPTER II

The Junior Pledge

Why do we have a pledge in the Junior society?

Because having our duty written out and placed definitely before us helps us. Also because we are helped by promising to do our duty; we are far more likely to do it than if we had not promised.

But is it not better not to promise than to promise and fail to keep the pledge?

Yes, but better than either is it to promise and to keep the promise! To be afraid of making promises is cowardly; it is a confession that we are weak.

How will keeping the Junior pledge help us all through our lives?

It will strengthen our wills, which are so powerful in making us successful in life. Besides, we are required to make many pledges in life, and being true to the Junior pledge will help us to be true to all these other pledges.

What is the first promise of the pledge?

That we will try to do whatever Christ would like to have us do. It is the broadest promise of the pledge.

How can we know what Christ would like to have us do?

By reading the Bible, which tells His will for us, and by praying and asking Him to make His will very plain to us. Also by getting the advice of older and wiser Christians, such as our parents and teachers and the Junior superintendent and the pastor.

Why do we promise to pray every day?

Because we need every day the strength and wisdom and comfort that prayer will give us. We talk every day with our earthly fathers; still more should we talk every day with our heavenly Father.

Why do we promise to read the Bible every day?

Because the Bible is our guide in life, and we need daily guidance for the tasks and perplexities of every day. The Bible is the food of our spirits, and we need to feed our spirits every day as well as our bodies.

What is meant by trying to lead a Christian life?

Just what is said in the first part of the pledge: that we will try to do what Christ wants us to do. We will let His will guide us in our work and play and talking and thinking and in every part of our lives, just so far as we know how.

What do we promise that refers to the Junior society?

To be present at every meeting when we can, and to take some part in every meeting.

What kind of taking part in the meeting will keep the pledge?

The kind that we think would be pleasing to Christ. He does not want our talking for Him and about Him to be a burden to us, and yet He does want us to grow in this power of Chris-

[15]

tian speech, as in all other powers. He wants us
to learn as soon as possible to talk to others
freely and easily and helpfully about religious
matters. Therefore we are to begin by reading
a verse, and then go on to repeat it from memory, and then add something of our own to it,
and then offer a sentence prayer, and so on. We
are to press on in prayer-meeting work in order
to become more useful Christians.

How can we be able to do all this?

As the first sentence of the pledge says,
"Trusting in the Lord Jesus Christ for strength."
If any part of the pledge seems hard, we have
only to remember that Christ with His infinite
wisdom and power is ready to help us keep it.

CHAPTER III

Christian Endeavor History and Principles

Who founded the Young People's Society of Christian Endeavor?

Rev. Francis E. Clark, at that time the pastor of the Williston Congregational Church in Portland, Maine.

When and where was it founded?

On the evening of February 2, 1881, in the parsonage of Williston Church.

Where and when was the second society formed?

In Newburyport, Massachusetts, in October of the same year.

Where and when was the first Christian Endeavor convention held?

It was held in Williston Church, in June, 1882, when only six societies were recorded.

What was the first Christian Endeavor book?

Dr. Clark's book, "Children and the Church," published in 1883.

When and where was the first Junior society formed?

On March 29, 1883, in the First Congregational Church of Berkeley, Cal., whose pastor was Rev. Charles A. Savage. Perhaps the second society was that formed in the Congregational Church of Tabor, Io., exactly a year later, the pastor being Rev. J. W. Cowan.

When and where was the national organization, the United Society of Christian Endeavor, formed?

At the national Convention held in Old Orchard, Maine, July, 1885.

When and where was the first Christian Endeavor local union formed?

In January, 1886, in New Haven, Connecticut.

When was the Christian Endeavor paper, "The Golden Rule," now "The Christian Endeavor World," established?

In October, 1886.

When did Dr. Clark become president of the United Society of Christian Endeavor, giving up from that time his entire life to the work?

In 1886.

When was Christian Endeavor Day, the birthday of our society, first observed?

In 1888.

When was the Junior paper, "The Junior Christian Endeavor World," established?

In January, 1893.

Who is the general secretary of the United Society?

Mr. William Shaw, who was one of the earliest members of the Christian Endeavor society.

At what national Christian Endeavor Convention was the first Junior rally held?

At that of New York City in 1892, when 35,000 Endeavorers came together.

In what cities have World's Christian Endeavor Conventions been held?

In Washington; London, England; Geneva,

Switzerland; and Agra, India. The next is in Sydney, Australia.

Where are Christian Endeavor societies to be found?

In every country of the globe, but especially in the United States, Great Britain, Germany, Canada, Brazil, South Africa, Australia, India, China, and Japan.

What are the leading principles of Christian Endeavor?

Pledged service of Christ. Regular witness-bearing for Christ. Daily prayer and Bible-reading. Loyalty to the church. Training in committee work. Fellowship with those of other churches.

Chapter IV

The President

What is the work of the Junior president?

To preside at the Junior business meetings and the meetings of the Junior executive committee, and to help the superintendent in the general management of the Junior society.

What is the first thing to do in the business meeting?

The president says, "The society will please come to order."

What comes next?

The president says, "The secretary will read the minutes of the last business meeting." Then, when the minutes have been read, the president asks: "Are there any corrections of the minutes?" If there are, the president instructs the secretary to make the corrections; and finally, in any case, the president says, "The minutes stand approved."

What comes next in order?

The reports of the secretary, and treasurer, and of the regular committees. The last will be made by the chairman of each committee. After each report the president says, "If there is no objection, the report will be placed on file"; when it will be handed to the secretary for preservation.

What follows next in order?

Unfinished business, for which the president will call. Under this head will come all matters left unfinished at the last meeting, including the reports of special committees, and whatever has been "laid on the table" for further consideration.

What is the final item of the business meetings?

New business, for which the president will call: "Is there any new business?" It will then be in order for any Junior to introduce any new proposal. The proper way is for the Junior to put his proposal in the form of a resolution: "Mr. President, I move that ———." The president will then say, "Is the motion seconded?" When it is seconded, the president will ask,

"Are there any remarks?" After all have spoken that wish to, the president will ask, "Are you ready for the motion? All in favor of the motion will say 'Aye'; contrary-minded, 'No,'" or, "All in favor will raise the hand. Contrary-minded, the same sign." The president will announce the result: "The motion is carried," (or, "The motion is lost").

What if a motion is made to amend the motion?

Then the motion to amend must be put first, and after it is carried the original motion must be put as it has been amended; if it is not carried, then the original motion must be put as it was made at first.

How is the business meeting closed?

The president asks, "Is there any more new business? If not, a motion to adjourn is in order." Some one moves that the society adjourn, and the motion is put in the usual way. If it is carried, the president says, "The society stands adjourned."

How are meetings of the executive committee conducted?

In the same way. The chairmen and officers present will report as they report to the society, but not in writing or so formally.

How will the president help the superintendent in managing the society?

The two will consult together all the time. The president will see that the other officers and the committees do their duty, and will aid the superintendent in all the ways suggested. But he will not do anything of importance without getting her advice and following it.

CHAPTER V

The Vice-President

What is the work of the vice-president?

To attend to the president's duties in his absence, and when he is present to help him in every way.

How can the vice-president learn what the president's duties are?

By watching the president. Also he will be asked by the president to act as president now and then, even when the president is in the meeting, so as to accustom him to the president's duties.

What if the president does not do this?

Then this chapter may be shown him, with the suggestion that he should do so occasionally.

How can the vice-president help the president in his work?

Part of the president's work is to see to the other officers and the committees and spur them on to do their full duty. The vice-president may arrange to do this for certain committees, and so relieve the president to that extent. For instance, he may arrange to be present at the meetings of the scrap-book committee and flower committee and music committee and birthday committee.

What will the vice-president do when he attends these committee meetings?

He will make suggestions for work that may be done, and will help the committee plan the work. To be able to do this the vice-president, like the president, should study the Junior work in many branches. Reading the different chapters of this book is the best way of doing this.

How can the vice-president help the president in the meetings of the Junior society?

He may sit on one side of the room and the president on the other side, and each will be ready to act as president on his side of the room. For instance, if a hymn is called for but in a voice that cannot be heard, the president or the vice-president may announce the number in a clear voice. If there is any disorder, the president and the vice-president may quietly stop it.

How can the vice-president help in the business meetings?

If a motion ought to be made and the Juniors hesitate about making it, the vice-president may make it. Whenever the meeting hitches in any way the vice-president may help it along.

How can the vice-president help in the meetings of the executive committee?

Once in a while, when the president invites him, he may preside over the committee meeting. At all times he may be ready with suggestions for plans of work and with praise of what has been done, to encourage the other Juniors.

How can the president and the vice-president be sure to work well together?

They should often talk over the work of the society together, and each should know what the other is trying to bring about. They should be real Christian Endeavor partners. Every true partnership greatly strengthens the partners,

and it will be this way with the president and
the vice-president.

**Will the vice-president be made president in
his turn?**

He may and he may not; that depends upon
many things. But, at any rate, he will be in
training to become president if the society and
the superintendent think best, and he will have
developed himself splendidly by his service as
vice-president.

CHAPTER VI

The Secretary

What are the duties of the Junior secretary?

To keep the minutes of the society business meetings and of the meetings of the executive committee. Also to keep the list of the members and a record of their attendance. Also to notify officers and committees of their election, and sometimes to carry on correspondence for the society.

What should the secretary put down in the minutes of the business meetings?

First, the statement that the society met on such a day in such a month and year and at such a time of day. Then, that the minutes of the last meeting were read and approved, with or without corrections, as the case may be. Then will follow an account of the reports of officers and committees, giving the most important points made by each. Then an account of whatever business is brought up, old or new. The minutes

will tell about all motions that were made and
carried, and it is also well to record, for the information of the society, the motions that were
made and not carried. If officers or new members
are elected, their names will be given.

**When will the secretary write out the notes
taken during the business meeting?**

Just as soon as possible, so that their meaning
will not be forgotten. They will not be written
out in the record-book of the society, however,
till they have been approved by the society.
Then they should be copied as soon as possible,
so as to be ready for reference. The secretary
will always take her record-book to the business
meetings, so as to tell the society, if asked, what
was done at any meeting.

**What will the secretary do when members are
voted in or officers or committees elected?**

The secretary will write a nice note to each
new member telling him that he has been elected
to membership in the society, and that you are
all glad and hope that he will get much good
from the society and give much that is good to

[30]

the society. To the chosen officers and committees the secretary will always write, telling each that at the last business meeting he was elected to such a place.

How will the secretary keep the list of names of the members?

The active members will be kept separate from the preparatory members.

Each will sign the constitution book and will place after his name the date of signing and the address—street and number. The birthday should also be written down, for the sake of the birthday committee.

How will the secretary call the roll at the consecration meetings?

For this purpose the secretary will have a separate book in which she will keep a record of attendance. Arrange the names in alphabetical order, but do not always call them in that order. Sometimes call them in irregular order, so that the Juniors will need to watch carefully to know when they should take part.

[31]

What is especially necessary for a secretary to do in calling the roll?

Speak very distinctly and promptly. Do not let it drag. Much of the success of the consecration meeting depends on the way the secretary calls the roll.

CHAPTER VII

The Treasurer

What is the duty of the Junior treasurer?

To take care of the money of the society and pay it out when called upon to do so by the proper persons.

How will the treasurer take care of the society's money?

It must be kept in a safe place and always kept separate from the treasurer's own money. The treasurer will never borrow from it, but will always be ready to hand it over — all of it — if the society wants it.

How will the treasurer keep account of the society's money?

He will have a society account-book and will enter on the left-hand page all the money he receives, and on the right-hand page all the money he pays out. The first page will be headed, "Receipts," and the second page, "Expenditures."

How will the receipts be entered?

Each receipt will be dated and will say from whom, or on what occasion, the money is received, and then will follow the amount, as:

Jan. 27. Monthly collection . . . $ .37
Apr. 6. Proceeds of the Junior enter-
          tainment 10.25

How will the expenditures be entered?

The date and person to whom, or the object to which, the money is given, and the amount; as:

Sept. 12. To Sarah Grant for expenses
        of the social Sept. 3 . . $1.50

Who will give orders for the treasurer to pay money from the treasury?

Your society constitution will tell. Usually it is best for the superintendent alone to give these orders.

How will the society money be obtained?

The best way is for each Junior to agree to give so much every month. Then give each Junior twelve little envelopes bearing the same number — a number placed opposite the Junior's name on the treasurer's record-book. At each

[34]

consecration meeting the Junior will put into the contribution-box one of his envelopes with the sum in it which he promised. The treasurer will enter the sum opposite his name.

How much should be given by each Junior?

Only what he and his parents can well afford; but urge that each Junior give something, if only a cent a month. The treasurer will tell the total amount received, but will not tell how much each Junior gives.

What if a Junior does not pay what he promises?

The treasurer will remind him of his failure at once, without waiting for the sums due to accumulate. He will say, "You have forgotten to bring your society dues, and I will call for the money, so that I can keep the treasury full."

What is the society "budget"?

It is a list made out at the beginning of the year of the different objects to which the society would like to give and the amount of money it expects to raise for each during the year. Include the society expenses in the budget. Make a reasonable budget, and then work hard to raise the full amount you set out to raise.

Who will lead the society in raising and earning the money?

The treasurer, with the help of the appropriate committees, such as the missionary and the social.

CHAPTER VIII

The Lookout Committee

Why is the lookout committee so called?

Because it looks out for all opportunities of improving the society.

What are the two directions in which the lookout committee is to look out?

It is to look out for new members, and it is to look out for the old members that they may be kept faithful.

How may the lookout committee look out for new members?

It may meet with the superintendent and make out a list of all the boys and girls that ought to join the Junior society. These names will be divided up among the members of the committee for each to invite to join the society.

What are the best ways of getting new members to join the society?

Tell them about the society, asking them if

[37]

they would not like to go to one of the meetings
and see how they enjoy it. Tell them that you
want them to join the society, if they will, after
they have seen what it is like. Then go after
them and bring them to the meeting, intro-
ducing them to the others and making them
have a good time.

**How can the committee make sure that the
new members are in earnest when they join?**

Be sure to show them the Junior pledge and
go over it sentence by sentence, explaining all
parts of it. The superintendent will help the
committee do this. It is best for the new members to come in first as preparatory members,
unless you are sure of their earnestness.

**What if one member of the committee fails to
win the boy or the girl whom you want to win?**

Then other members of the committee will
make the attempt, or other members of the
society, till some one succeeds.

**How may the committee set the new mem-
bers to work?**

Get the prayer-meeting committee to give them some definite work to do in the prayer meeting. See that they are placed upon some committee. Give them some part in preparing for the next social. See that the other members of the society take them in and make them feel at home.

How can the lookout committee keep the members of the society faithful?

Divide up the members of the society among the members of the committee, each to keep a record of the attendance of those assigned to him, and of their participation in each meeting. Send a copy of this record to each member once a month.

How can the committee remind the members of their pledge?

By having a copy of the pledge hung before the society. By having the pledge repeated in every consecration meeting. By seeing that each member of the society has a private copy of the pledge hung in his or her sleeping-room. By having different Juniors write and read two-

[39]

minute essays on the different sections of the pledge, one section at each consecration meeting.

What can the lookout committee do for the preparatory members?

It can divide them among the members of the committee, like the active members, and watch that they are regular in attendance. It can urge them to take some simple part in the meetings and go on to harder parts.

CHAPTER IX

The Prayer-Meeting Committee

What is the work of the prayer-meeting committee?

To arrange for the prayer meetings, and to do all it can to make the prayer meetings successful.

Who should lead the meetings?

All of the active members, in time, and as fast as they can be trained to do it.

What are some ways of training the leaders?

Those that are at first too timid to lead a meeting by themselves may be willing to lead with an older member, the two sitting together before the society and the timid member doing the easier parts of the leading. After a while the timid member will become willing to lead by himself or herself.

How can the prayer-meeting committee help the members to take part in the meetings?

By copying the questions given in *The*

Junior Christian Endeavor World and giving them out for the Juniors to answer. In *The Junior Christian Endeavor World* topics are also given for them to speak upon, and these should be given to the older Juniors. Thoughts are also given for the Juniors to tell in their own words, adding what they can of their own thoughts, and these will be copied and given out by the committee.

What use will the committee make of Bible verses?

It will sometimes give out Bible verses a week in advance, asking the Juniors to commit them to memory and repeat them in the meeting. The committee will ask the more experienced Juniors to add some thought of their own to the verses.

How will the committee help the Juniors to put more prayers into the meetings?

The committee may call for sentence prayers and start them themselves. A member of the committee will simply say, "Will not many follow me in sentence prayers?" Then a member of the committee will offer a sentence prayer,

[42]

and the other members of the committee will follow promptly.

What are prayer trios?

Two members of the committee will arrange with some beginner that one of the committee will offer a brief prayer, then the beginner will pray, and then the other member of the committee will pray. Thus the beginner will be sandwiched in between two others.

What else will the committee do for the prayer meeting?

It may give out a recitation appropriate to the subject and have it repeated in the meeting. Every week *The Christian Endeavor World* gives such a recitation. One of the committee may give a chalk-talk. The pictures are given every week in *The Christian Endeavor World*, and many Juniors actually copy them and give a little talk about them before the society. An outline object-talk is also given in *The Christian Endeavor World* each week, and a little anecdote to be told, and these also will be used.

[43]

How may the committee introduce older speakers?

Of course the committee in all its plans will leave room for the superintendent's talk, and indeed the entire plan will be made out in consultation with the superintendent. When the superintendent thinks it best, the committee may invite some older person to come and give a brief talk to the Juniors—the pastor or the Sunday-school superintendent or some parent or a member of the older Christian Endeavor society.

CHAPTER X

The Missionary Committee

What, in brief, is the work of the Junior missionary committee?

To conduct the Junior missionary meetings, or at least help in every way to make them successful; and to further an interest in missions among the Juniors.

What is a good way to plan for the Junior missionary meetings?

Divide the society into Junior missionary bands, one for each missionary meeting of the year, and let each band study to make its meeting the best of the year. The missionary committee members may divide themselves among these bands, each to superintend one of them and lead its meeting.

What are some features that should be in most, if not all, missionary meetings?

The map should be used freely, all places mentioned being pointed out. A free use should be made of pictures, and all that can be found that bear on the subject of the meeting should be placed on the wall or passed around for the inspection of the Juniors. Always the work done by your own denomination in the land under discussion should be described.

What use should be made of clippings about missionary fields?

They should be used freely, but every effort should be made to have the Juniors repeat from memory what they contain as well as they can, and never read them. To give only a small part of a clipping in one's own words is far better than to read it all.

How will missionary clippings be gathered?

They may be collected by the scrap-book committee as well as the missionary committee. They will be obtained from missionary and other religious periodicals, and many good things may be copied from books. They will be preserved in a series of envelopes, one for each of the missionary countries, and others for different branches of home-mission work, such as

Indians, negroes, Chinese in America, emigrants, home-mission schools, city missions.

How will pictures be kept?

They also will be gathered from the same sources, and picture postal cards will also be collected. These will be kept in envelopes, classified like the clippings.

What will the committee do in regard to the missionary magazines?

There are missionary papers and magazines for children in several denominations, and there is *Everyland*, a magazine of foreign missions for all denominations. Also there is much for Juniors in the grown-up missionary periodicals. The missionary committee will get subscribers for the children's magazines and will lend them around among the members, marking the most interesting parts.

What will the committee do to interest the Juniors in missionary books?

It will itself read the missionary books and will recommend to the Juniors those that it

[47]

finds most interesting. Especially it will call attention to the missionary books in the Sunday-school and public library.

What are some missionary lives in which Juniors will be especially interested?

Those of Livingstone, Carey, John Williams, Alexander Mackay, James Chalmers, John G. Paton, James Gilmour, Henry Martyn, Marcus Whitman, and Dr. Grenfell. Most of these are specially written for children.

CHAPTER XI

The Social Committee

What is the social committee to do?

It is to plan the Junior socials with the superintendent, and help in carrying them out. It is
also to help the superintendent in welcoming
new members and making them feel at home,
and in the rest of the social life of the society.

How often should Junior socials be held?

That depends upon how many other social
entertainments the members of the society
have. As many socials should be held as seem
to be needed to keep the members interested
and to join them pleasantly together.

Where should the socials be held?

In the church vestry, if that is a good place
and the church is in favor of its being used in
that way. In any case it is well often to hold
the Junior socials in the homes of the members,
in order to get the home feeling.

When should the socials be held?

Preferably in the afternoon; if they are held in the evening it is hard to plan for getting the Juniors safely home, and they are likely to stay up too late.

Should refreshments be served at Junior socials?

If it can easily be arranged, simple refreshments will add much to the interest of the Juniors; but the refreshments should be very simple and inexpensive, such as nuts and apples, or cake and lemonade or home-made water ice.

How will the committee plan the socials?

Very thoroughly, so that nothing will be left to chance or to the decision of the moment, but every part of the time will be laid out in advance. Have a definite written programme.

What should come first in a social?

Some game that brings in everybody in a simple way, such as gathering the autographs of all present, a little reward being given to the one that gathers the most in a certain time. The first game is for the purpose of getting the strangers acquainted.

What kinds of games are to be played?

Those that are sensible. Of course, no kissing games. Games of skill, that bring out the ability of the members. These are far more interesting than the silly games in which thoughtless young people indulge. For example, "proverbs" is a good game; so is "throwing the handkerchief," because it depends upon bodily activity; so is "twenty questions," or "clumps."

How should a social be ended?

Right at the appointed time for closing. Gather the Juniors together and have them sing a well-known hymn, and then the superintendent will offer a prayer and the social will be ended.

Who will be invited to the social?

All the Juniors, active and preparatory members. Also the Junior committee of the older society, if there is one. Also the pastor and his wife. Sometimes the society will give a social to the parents of the Juniors, with some entertainment in which they can join. Once a year a social may be held for boys and girls that are not members of the society, just to get them interested in the society and lead them to attend the meetings and at last to join.

What other social work will the social committee do?

It will see that there are no lonely or "left out" members in the Junior society, and it will do its best to break up all "cliques" and "sets." These have no place in a society of young Christians. Its aim will be to illustrate in every way Christ's spirit of brotherly and sisterly love.

Chapter XII

The Music Committee

What is the work of the music committee?

To improve the singing of the society and to do what it can for the music of the society in general.

How will the music committee help the prayer meetings?

By getting up special music and by getting the Juniors to sing more heartily.

What special music may the committee get up?

It will get different Juniors to sing solos now and then. These solos may be simply hymns; but whatever they are, they should be suited to the subject of the meeting. If, for instance, it is a missionary or a temperance meeting, the solos should be missionary hymns or temperance hymns.

What other special singing may be introduced?

[53]

Duets or quartettes or choruses. These will be carefully practised well in advance.

What instrumental music may be obtained by the committee?

Some of the Juniors may play the violin or the violoncello or the cornet, and other instruments, and they will give solos or accompany the singing. Others will play upon the piano or organ. Indeed, sometimes the drum may be used, or the fife.

What about whistling?

Many Junior superintendents have the boys whistle the tunes now and then, and if it is done reverently it produces a fine effect.

What larger musical organizations may be formed?

A Junior orchestra, bringing together all the Juniors that play musical instruments. A Junior choir, bringing together all that sing. These should be trained by good leaders.

What use may be made of the Junior singers and orchestra outside the Junior meetings?

They may now and then be used in the church services, and they may play in entertainments of different kinds, at outdoor gatherings, and in public institutions. There will be many occasions when they will be useful.

How may the Juniors be made familiar with their song-book?

You may have musical socials now and then at which singing is the principal feature. At these socials sing mainly the songs in your hymnal with which you are not familiar. You will make many new friends.

What are some ways of giving variety to the singing?

Have the prayer songs sung with bowed heads. Sometimes have a few singers go out of the room and repeat each stanza of a hymn after the society has sung it; this "echo" will be most pleasing. Sometimes have the boys sing a stanza and the girls the next stanza. Sometimes have the right and left halves of the society sing alternate stanzas. Sometimes have a hymn read in concert by all the Juniors before it is sung. Sometimes have a marching hymn sung while the society marches around the room. Sometimes have the society commit hymns to memory. *The Junior Christian Endeavor World* gives a memory hymn every month, telling about the writer of it. Have the committees choose committee hymns, and have the society choose a consecration hymn which it will sing at all the consecration meetings of the year.

CHAPTER XIII

The Flower Committee

What is the flower committee to do?

It is to provide flowers for the church, when this work is not done by some other organization. It is to provide flowers for the Junior meetings, and take them afterwards to the sick and to others. It is to make use of flowers in other helpful ways.

Where will the flower committee get its flowers?

From the homes of the members. It may buy them in the winter, if it can get money for the purpose.

How may the flower committee get money for flowers?

If it furnishes flowers for the church, it will call upon the older church-members to supply money for them, at least during the time of year when they cannot be obtained in the gardens and the fields. The society may give flower entertainments for raising money, or earn it in other ways.

How may the committee and the society raise flowers?

Each member of the committee may have a flower garden for the purpose, or, at least, a flower-bed which he will tend. The members of the society may each be given one package of flower-seed to raise. Bulbs may be distributed among the members, to be raised and brought to the church when in bloom. The different members may agree to raise different kinds of house plants for the decoration of the church. Also the committee will find out what members of the congregation have house plants that can be used for the church, and when they will be in blossom.

How may the committee stimulate the raising of flowers?

By holding an annual exhibition of flowers and plants raised by the members, and offering rewards for the best gardens and best flower-beds and the best plants of different kinds.

What from the fields and the woods will the committee use for decoration?

Wild vines, branches of bright leaves, stalks of corn and sheaves of wheat, bunches of fruit, branches full of bright berries, evergreen boughs, and all kinds of wild flowers.

What may the committee do for the church yard?

It may cultivate flower-beds there, and keep the lawn and the walks neatly. All this will be done under the supervision of the proper church officers.

What use will the committee make of the flowers after the Sunday services are over?

They will take them to the sick and the aged, and to all whom the society wishes to honor. The flowers will be given on the occasion of birthdays and other anniversaries.

How may the flowers be used as rewards?

They may be given to the Juniors that have attended without fail for three months at a time; also to those that have brought in new members, and to the new members themselves; also to those that lead the meeting for the first time, and to others that have done special work.

What should always go with the flowers?

Some message from the committee telling who sent the flowers and why they are sent, and adding some expression of the society's good will and love. Moreover, the committee will take the flowers in person, and will not merely send them by some unsympathetic messenger.

CHAPTER XIV

The Information Committee

What is the object of the information committee?

To tell the Juniors about interesting Christian Endeavor events in all parts of the world, and about new methods in Junior Christian Endeavor work; also to give interesting news about your denomination and its work, at home and abroad, and the progress of Christ's Kingdom everywhere.

Why is this committee important?

Because the Juniors will not be enthusiastic for Christian Endeavor unless they know about it; and the more they know about it, the better they will work for it.

How large should the committee be?

It may have only one member, if yours is a small society; or it may have as many as three members, or more.

How often should the committee report?

As a rule, at every prayer meeting; but if any meeting is sure to be crowded, the report of the information committee may be omitted. The report may best come after the opening song and before the leader's remarks on the topic.

Who will call for the report of the committee?

The leader should have a written order of exercises, in which the report of this committee is set down. If by any mistake the report is not called for, the chairman of the committee will rise and say, "The information committee has not given its report."

When the committee has several members, who should make the report?

The members of the committee will report, taking turns. The chairman will see that this is done, and, besides taking his turn, he may sometimes add to the report made by another member of the committee.

How long a report should be given?

Never longer than five minutes; much less

than that, if the news does not call for **five** minutes. Do not pad it.

Where will the committee get its information?

From the Christian Endeavor and other religious papers. *The Junior Christian Endeavor World* contains in every number a supply of Christian Endeavor news paragraphs written especially for this committee, two or more for each meeting of the month.

What kinds of news items should be chosen?

Those that will interest the Juniors. Do not often select accounts of meetings, for those are so much alike that they do not arouse interest. Often report new and good plans that the society can carry out.

In what way should the report be given?

The speaker will get far better attention if he comes forward and faces the society. He will never read from a paper, but he will get the facts well fixed in his mind and tell them to the society in his own words. He should be brisk, and there will be no harm in adding a bit of fun

[63]

now and then. He will speak clearly and earnestly. He will be practical, and will apply his information to the needs of his own society. He should practise making his report before he comes to the meeting.

What are some different ways of making the report?

Sometimes all three members will stand before the society, and each in turn will give a brief report. Sometimes the report will be printed in big letters on a large sheet of paper and placed before the society. Sometimes the speaker will ask the Juniors to repeat after him the information he has just given, so as to impress it on their minds. Sometimes the speaker will ask questions on the information given for a month back, to see whether the society remembers it. Sometimes the committee, for several months, will give information each week about **Christian Endeavor** work in a different country.

CHAPTER XV

The Temperance Committee

How large may the Junior temperance committee be?

It may consist of only a single member, if the society is not large enough to have a larger committee.

What is the work of the committee?

To conduct the Junior temperance meetings, or, at least, help in carrying them on, if the committee is not large enough to conduct all of them. Also to do what it can to arouse in the society an interest in temperance and give knowledge about temperance.

Where will the temperance committee get its facts?

From the annual temperance almanacs and handbooks and from the weekly and monthly temperance papers; also from books about temperance and the lives of workers for temperance.

[65]

How will the temperance committee get the Juniors interested in temperance reading?

By lending these books and magazines with the most interesting parts marked. By finding interesting temperance stories in the Sunday-school library and the public library and telling the society about them.

How can the temperance committee keep the subject of temperance before the society?

By taking, with the superintendent's permission, one minute or more at each Junior meeting to give ·one temperance fact or anecdote.

What use may be made of temperance pictures?

There are many effective temperance pictures, including cartoons, diagrams, and charts. These may be cut out by the committee and mounted on pasteboard, to hang in the Junior room or to pass around among the members.

What use may be made of temperance mottoes?

Striking facts bearing on temperance may be

[66]

printed on placards and hung in the Junior room. These should be changed as soon as the Juniors become familiar with them.

What use will be made of song by the committee?

There are bright temperance song-books for sale by the Women's Christian Temperance Union and the National Temperance Society. The committee may get up a temperance chorus to sing these at the society meetings.

How will the temperance committee use the pledge?

Temperance pledges will be distributed among the members for all to sign that will. Make a list of the signers. A society temperance pledge may be made, to be framed and hung in the Junior room, signed by all the members and by the new members as they join the society. Some societies will prefer a pledge-book instead of a wall pledge.

How will the temperance committee make the temperance meetings of the society shine?

[67]

Prepare for them long in advance. Arm all the Juniors with temperance facts for them to repeat in the meeting. Have temperance poems recited and temperance songs sung. Exhibit temperance charts and pictures, with explanations. Have a Junior give an account of the life of some great temperance worker, like Miss Willard or John B. Gough. Get some strong outside speaker to talk to the society. Have many prayers for temperance.

CHAPTER XVI

The Good-Literature Committee

What work should a Junior good-literature committee do?

It should try to get the members of the society to read good books, papers, and magazines.

Who should be members of the committee?

The boys and girls that like to read the best books and periodicals, and will be active in recommending them to others.

What papers and magazines will the good-literature committee urge the Juniors to read?

The Junior Christian Endeavor World, and the children's papers and magazines published by your denomination, especially those of the missionary boards. It will also call attention to especially helpful stories, articles, and poems in the religious periodicals for adults and in secular periodicals.

How will the good-literature committee add to the circulation of these periodicals?

By getting up clubs for them. Send for sample copies and for terms to agents and premium lists. Lend the sample copies among your friends. Speak about the papers in the society meetings. Sometimes you may read in the society meetings bits of especially good articles. Keep sample copies hung up in the society meeting-place, each marked with the subscription price. Call from house to house, seeking subscribers. Often you will be most successful if you go right to the parents of the children, for they have the money to spend.

What kinds of books will the committee try to get the Juniors to read?

The best stories, those that make the readers better Christians. Lives of the noblest men, especially of the great missionaries. Books about this beautiful world, and God's work in it. Books about the Bible, and books about our country.

How will the Juniors get the books that the committee recommends as worth reading?

The committee will name some that can be found in the Sunday-school library, and others that are in the public library. You may get up a Junior library, giving entertainments to raise money for the books. Arrangements may be made for lending good books among the Juniors, the books to be passed from one to another in a certain order, and kept by each Junior for one or two weeks.

How will the committee get the Juniors interested in good books?

A member of the committee, after reading a book and becoming enthusiastic about it, will tell the society a little about it at a society meeting, holding it up. Ask on the spot what Junior would like to read it, and hand it over at once.

How is a reading-contest conducted?

The committee will offer some reward, perhaps a book, which will be given to the Junior who reads in six months the largest number of books and the best-selected list.

[71]

What can the good-literature committee do to help others to good reading-matter?

It can gather up the books, magazines, and papers that the Juniors have read, and can send or take them to children's hospitals, orphans' homes, and other places.

What are reading-circles?

Groups of Juniors, organized by the good-literature committee, who will meet at the homes of the members, each group to read some book which it has selected under the guidance of the superintendent.

What will the good-literature committee gain from this work?

A better knowledge of books and a deeper love for good reading. Both of these are invaluable.

Chapter XVII

The Birthday Committee

What is the duty of the birthday committee?

To keep a list of the birthdays of the Juniors, both active and preparatory members, of the superintendent, pastor, pastor's wife, and all others whom the society may wish to honor on their birthdays. The committee will see that these birthdays are properly observed.

How will this list be arranged?

In the order of the days, so that the committee can tell at a glance just what birthdays come next.

How will the birthdays be observed in the meetings?

The committee will give a report when the superintendent calls for it, saying, "The birthdays of Robert Jones, Mary Clements, and Francis Hannay come this week." They will name the birthdays that take place during the

[73]

seven days to come, not the birthdays of the past seven days.

What will be done next after this report?

The superintendent may offer a prayer for these Juniors, or she may call upon some member of the birthday committee to pray for them. The superintendent may give them a little word of advice for the new year of their lives.

How may the birthdays be celebrated by music?

The society may choose a birthday hymn to be sung at all such times during the year. Or the Juniors whose birthdays come during the week may each choose a hymn which will be their hymn for the year, and one verse of each hymn (or more verses if you have time) may be sung by the society.

What use may be made of birthday mottoes?

The birthday committee may choose a year's motto for each of the Juniors whose birthdays are being celebrated, and may give these mottoes to them when the superintendent calls upon them to do so. Then each Junior whose birthday is celebrated will read his motto aloud. Or, the committee may get the Juniors to select their own mottoes for the year and bring them to the meeting to announce. It will be pleasant if the committee can print out the mottoes neatly on heavy cardboard, so that the Juniors may hang them up in their rooms.

What use may be made of flowers?

The flowers with which the flower committee has decorated the room may be given to the Juniors whose birthdays are celebrated. This use of flowers is especially suitable if you are celebrating the birthday of your pastor or his wife or the Junior superintendent.

What birthday gifts may be made?

Each Junior whose birthday is celebrated may be asked to bring to the meeting as many pennies as he or she is years old, and drop them into the contribution-box, one by one, while the society counts aloud.

What gifts may be made to those whose birthdays you are celebrating?

[75]

The society may have a fund to which each member may give ten cents from which ten-cent presents may be bought for each Junior on his birthday. Some helpful little book would be appropriate. Special collections may be made to buy birthday presents for the pastor and his wife and the superintendent; but if that is done, no one should be allowed to give more than one cent. It is not the cost of the gift that counts, but the love that goes with it; and our societies must not do anything in which the poorest Junior cannot easily join.

CHAPTER XVIII

The Sunshine Committee

What is the work of the sunshine committee?

To do any helpful, cheering, loving deed that the members can think of.

What if the deed you think of falls naturally to the hands of another committee?

Then suggest it to that committee and offer to help in doing it, if your help is wanted. If after a while it is not done, then your committee may do it.

Who are to suggest the things the sunshine committee may do?

Any member of the committee, and the superintendent. You should also ask for suggestions from the pastor, from your parents, from the older church workers, and from all friends and helpers of the society.

Whom will the sunshine committee especially seek to help and cheer?

The sick, especially sick children and the sick of the Junior society. The poor, especially poor children. Those in hospitals and asylums and almshouses and homes for the aged. Those that are lonely. Old people that are confined to the house or to their rooms. Strangers in the town and in the church. Foreigners, especially the poor among the emigrants.

What can the sunshine committee do for the sick?

It can visit them, when they are able to see visitors and their parents think it is best. It can sing in the hospitals. It can help the flower committee take flowers to the sick. It can carry fruit and jelly and other good things to sick-rooms. It can play games with those that are getting well but are still confined to the house.

What can the sunshine committee do with pictures?

It can lend the most beautiful pictures it can find, placing them on the walls of sick-rooms, and moving them from house to house as they become familiar.

What can the sunshine committee do with books?

Its members can take their own favorite books and lend them to those that are shut in and will enjoy them. The same thing can be done with magazines. Often the sick one will not be able to read, but will enjoy hearing some Junior read aloud.

What can the sunshine committee do with song?

They can cheer the aged by singing outside their homes or in their houses. Call these visits "serenades." Never make such a visit unless you have been assured by some member of the household that the visit will be welcome.

What can be done with letters?

Sometimes when you cannot see those whom you would like to help you can write them jolly letters which will do them almost as much good as visits would do. The committee may join together in writing these letters.

[79]

How may the sunshine committee help the poor?

By collecting food and clothing and giving it out. By gathering up toys for the children, and other things to make them happy. All this work will be done under the advice and with the aid of some wise grown-up who knows the real needs of the poor and how to help them without hurting them.

In what spirit will the sunshine committee work?

In the loving spirit of Jesus; and working in His spirit, they will be indeed a blessing.

CHAPTER XIX

The Scrap-Book Committee

What is the work of the Junior scrap-book committee?

To aid the society in every way with the use of clippings and scrap-books and similar things.

What scrap-books will the committee keep for the other committees?

It will start and keep up a set of committee scrap-books, one for each of the committees. In these scrap-books the committee will gather up the methods of work it can find for the different committees. *The Junior Christian Endeavor World*, for instance, prints in every number some method of work for each of the principal Junior committees, and these in the course of the year make twelve methods for each committee. *The Christian Endeavor World* also has very many methods for Junior societies.

What help may the committee give to the missionary committee?

[81]

It may make a set of missionary scrap-books, one book for each missionary country, full of interesting facts and pictures relating to that country. Sometimes it will be best to put these clippings into a set of envelopes, one for each country, so that they can be given out separately to the Juniors.

How may the scrap-book committee help the flower committee?

It may make a collection of beautiful extracts in prose and poetry and may paste these on cards. The flower committee will write personal messages on the cards and will send them with their flowers to the sick and others.

How may the scrap-book committee aid the sunshine committee?

It may make scrap-books for the hospitals, and for the sick of the Junior society and the congregation. These scrap-books should be very light, consisting of only a few sheets fastened together, and perhaps each of only a single sheet. Thus the committee may make sheets of jokes, sheets

[82]

of lovely poems, sheets each of which contains a pleasant story, sheets of funny pictures, and so on.

How may the scrap-book committee use Christmas cards, Easter cards, and the like?

It may cover fans with them for the sick. It may cover screens with them. It may put them together for the covers of their scrap-books. It may tie them in bunches to be given out, a dozen at a time.

What will the scrap-book committee do with the chapters of serials?

It may cut them out, fold them, and place them all together in an envelope, properly marked. These envelopes will be much prized in sick-rooms.

How may the scrap-book committee help the temperance committee?

By making collections of temperance articles, long and short, and temperance poems and stories, giving them to the temperance committee for use in their work.

[83]

How may the scrap-book committee help the prayer-meeting committee?

By keeping in mind the topics of the coming meetings, and setting aside for the use of the prayer-meeting committee all the poems and prose extracts and anecdotes that bear on the prayer-meeting topics.

How will the scrap-book committee get material for its work?

It will gather up from the homes of the members all the old papers and magazines it can find. It will soon discover what periodicals give it the best material, and part of the gain that will come to the committee will be this knowledge of periodicals.

How will the committee get its work done?

It will meet regularly once a month for delightful evenings with the scissors and the paste-brush.

CHAPTER XX

Junior Prayer-Meeting Leaders

What is the work of the prayer-meeting leader?

To plan the meetings, with the help of the superintendent, and then to do what he can to make the meetings successful.

When should the leader begin his preparation?

As soon as he learns that he is to lead the meeting. He should at once read the verses chosen for the meeting and fix the subject of the meeting well in mind, so that he can think about it at odd minutes and get ideas for it.

What should the leader put into his opening words at the meeting?

Just one thought about the subject. He may write this out and read it, but it is far better if he has it in mind so well that he can speak it without having it written. That makes it seem to come more from his own life. This opening talk should be very simple—no more than the Junior would say if he were not leading.

For what else will the leader prepare?

He will make out a list of hymns to be sung (with the help of the music committee, if his society has one). He will read the special directions for the meeting in *The Junior Christian Endeavor World*, and will carry out the suggestions made there as far as they fit his society.

What will be most helpful in planning a meeting?

To introduce one feature that is new. It may not be wholly new, but it should not have been used for a long time. This novelty will freshen up the entire meeting and increase the interest of the members in it. You will find many suggestions for such plans in the committee department of *The Junior Christian Endeavor World* under the heading, "For Prayer-Meeting Committees," and also in the prayer-meeting department under the heading, "For Junior Leaders."

[86]

What is most necessary for the leader to do in beginning the meeting?

Begin promptly on time, and in a bright, strong way that means business. Take hold of the meeting with vigor and it is likely to move with vigor all through.

What is most necessary for the leader to remember in carrying out his programme for the meeting?

To move briskly from one point to the next without hesitating and delaying. Have a programme that will fill the hour full, and then push your programme rapidly so that it will not stretch out beyond the hour.

What are some features that should be in nearly all prayer meetings?

Sentence prayers, giving all a chance to contribute very brief prayers to a chain of prayers. Singing, bright and cheery, and lots of it. Something about the topic from as many of the members as will contribute. Leave a lot of room for this. The answering of written questions on the subject, which the leader will obtain from *The*

Junior Christian Endeavor World and give out to the members. Also some additional feature, like a recitation or a vocal solo or a blackboard talk. And, of course, the superintendent's talks and drills will be included.

What will be the best help the Junior leader can have in his leading?

Prayer. Ask God to help you, and He will be sure to do so. He will help you in getting something to say, if you are industrious; and He will help you to plan the meeting, if you will do your part toward getting plans; and He will help by putting His spirit into the meeting so that it will be a great success. Rely upon Him.

Chapter XXI

The Preparatory Members

What are the preparatory members of the Junior Christian Endeavor society?

They are those that wish to attend the meetings and promise to behave while there.

Why are they called preparatory members?

Because they are preparing to become active members. They do not intend to remain preparatory members very long.

Why are the preparatory members to attend the Junior meetings regularly?

Because that is the only way to learn about the Junior society and work into its ways so as to become able to be a good active member.

Why must the preparatory member promise to behave in the Junior meetings?

Because if he is not orderly and attentive he cannot get good from the meetings, and he will be preventing others from getting good. If he does not behave, it is a sign that he does not really wish to be a true Christian Endeavorer.

[89]

What is another name for preparatory members?

"Trial members," because they are on trial to see whether they really have any place in the Junior Christian Endeavor society and deserve membership in it.

Should the preparatory members take part in the Junior meetings?

Yes, in a quiet, modest way, and as soon as possible. That is the only way in which they and the superintendent can tell whether they are ready for active membership or not.

How should the preparatory member begin to take part?

By reading a verse from the Bible, or some other quotation. This quotation should be read over often at home, so that the preparatory member is very familiar with it and can read it without making a mistake. It should be read clearly and loudly so that all may hear.

How will the preparatory member go on in his preparation?

He may after a while commit to memory his Bible verse or other quotation and repeat it in the meeting. Then he may offer a little sentence prayer when prayers are called for. The best way is to commit to memory one of the Bible prayers, perhaps a verse from some Psalm, and repeat that as a prayer.

What committee work may the preparatory member do?

He may be placed upon a Junior committee to help the active members in it. Here he will do the best he can, and try to do as well as the active members.

What work will not be given to the preparatory members?

They will not be made leaders of meetings or chairmen of committees. Only active members are given such work.

What will the preparatory members do in the consecration meetings?

They will be ready to answer, "Present," when their names are called at the roll-call; in some societies, however, their names are not called at all — only the names of the active members. As soon as possible they will add something to this response of "Present," and that will be one sign that they are ready for active membership.

[91]

Who is to say when the preparatory member is ready to be an active member?

The superintendent. She will watch the preparatory members, and she is eager to advance them just as soon as they are ready for it.

CHAPTER XXII

The Quiet Hour

What is meant by the Quiet Hour?

It is a regular time spent every day in reading the Bible and thinking about it and about our lives, and in praying to God and hearing what He has to say to us.

How is the Quiet Hour connected with our Junior pledge?

In the pledge we promise to pray and read the Bible every day and to try to lead Christian lives. The Quiet Hour is to help us to do these things.

What are the Comrades of the Quiet Hour?

An organization established by Dr. Clark. The United Society of Christian Endeavor enrolls as Comrades of the Quiet Hour all that make it a rule of their lives to spend some definite part of every day—at least fifteen minutes—in quiet Bible-reading and prayer.

At what time should the Quiet Hour be observed?

At some regular time every day. Early in the morning is the best time.

How does one become a Comrade of the Quiet Hour?

Write to Rev. Francis E. Clark, Tremont Temple, Boston, saying that you would like to be a Comrade of the Quiet Hour and enclosing a two-cent stamp. The Quiet Hour covenant will be returned to you. You will sign it and keep it.

Where should the Quiet Hour be kept?

In the same place, as a rule, because being in that place will come to suggest good thoughts to you and put you in the right mood for the Quiet Hour.

Why is it best to observe the Quiet Hour early in the morning?

Because your mind is fresh then and you can think better. Besides, your prayers and Bible-reading can then be carried right into the work of the day to help you in it.

Is it all right to observe the Quiet Hour at night?

Yes, if you cannot well observe it in the morning. In that case you will think about what has happened in the day and pray for God's blessing on the next day.

Why is it best to keep the Quiet Hour for at least fifteen minutes?

The word "hour" does not mean a literal hour, but a "period." At least fifteen minutes is not too much, surely, to talk with our dear Father in heaven, who is doing all things for us.

How should we begin our Quiet Hours?

By reminding ourselves that our heavenly Father is in the room with us and that He is ready to hear whatever we have to say to Him and help us in all our troubles and answer all our prayers in the best way. Then we are to talk with Him about the things that concern us most deeply.

Why should we read the Bible in our Quiet Hours?

Because the Bible is God's letter to us. It is the book which He has given us for our guide in life. We shall make no mistake if we follow its teachings.

What are the gains from following the Quiet Hour?

We shall be stronger for all our duties and we shall enjoy all our pleasures more because we shall be closer to Jesus.

CHAPTER XXIII

The Tenth Legion

What is the Tenth Legion?

It is an enrollment of all those that make it a practice to set apart at least one-tenth of their income and use it for religious work.

How was the Tenth Legion started?

It was founded by Mr. W. L. Amerman in the New York City Christian Endeavor Union, and was soon adopted by the United Society of Christian Endeavor as a world-wide movement for generous giving.

What is the meaning of the name?

It refers to a great and powerful band of soldiers led by Julius Cæsar, the famous Roman general. It was called "The Tenth Legion." It is hoped that the legion of those that give the tenth will do as much for the kingdom of heaven as Cæsar's legion did for his earthly kingdom.

Why did the ancient Jews give a tenth?

[97]

They gave a tenth (or a tithe—the word means the same) to keep up the services in the Temple and for other purposes. Often they gave as much as three-tenths of their income.

Why should modern Christians give a tenth?

We are not under Jewish law, but we surely should do as much as the Jews did for our religion, which is so much better than theirs.

But ought not all Christians to give to God all that they have?

Yes, in a sense; that is, all that we have should be used in the way God wants us to use it, because He gave it all to us; but of course He does not expect us to use it all in distinctively religious work. But if we set apart one-tenth for religious work, it will help us to use all our money in the way He wants us to.

How is it like Sunday?

We are to keep all our time sacred to God and use it all in the way He wants us to use it; but we set apart one-seventh of our time for definite religious uses so that we may use all our time in the right way. Just so, setting apart one-tenth of our money for definite religious purposes helps us to use it all in the right way.

What is meant by "income"?

All the money that "comes in," whether it is given to us or we earn it, and whether it comes in regularly or irregularly.

What if it is given us to use for religious purposes, as for Sunday-school and Junior collections?

Then, of course, we are to use for that purpose all that is so given.

How may we join the Tenth Legion?

Write to General Secretary William Shaw, Tremont Temple, Boston, telling him you want to join, and sending a two-cent stamp. He will return the Tenth Legion certificate, which you are to keep.

Who is to decide how the tenth will be used?

You are to decide, with the advice of your

parents and Junior superintendent. Use it for whatever you think to be the purposes that are closest to Christ's heart.

www.ingramcontent.com/pod-product-compliance
Lightning Source LLC
Chambersburg PA
CBHW020510030426
42337CB00011B/313